Movements in Jars

Meghan Jackson

Movements in Jars

Meghan Jackson

CHAUDIERE BOOKS

cover design - Tanya Sprowl
author photo - Laura Kupcis
designed by Jennifer Mulligan
edited for the press by rob mclennan

printed and bound in Canada
by Custom Printers, Renfrew, Ontario

Chaudiere Books
858 Somerset Street West
Main Floor
Ottawa, Ontario
K1A 0R2

www.chaudierebooks.com
email: info@chaudierebooks.com

Library and Archives Canada Cataloguing in Publication

Jackson, Meghan
Movements in jars / Meghan Jackson.

Poems.
ISBN-13: 978-0-9781601-0-4
ISBN-10: 0-9781601-0-X

I. Title.

PS8619.A245M68 2006 C811'.6 C2006-905829-6

For Nicholas Jackson

with love, today, tomorrow, and always

Movements in Jars

fish: five tanka

taking green photo
graphs i notice silent frost
the tail curled stretching
tries to flip over solid fly
and speckled speckled grey

in the backyard smothered
with pine needles rust and fences
i sit on cement square
wet touches take oatmeal
from my cold fingers

i walk blue windows
past gurgling and coloured rocks
i've seen it before
don't look this time no time for
fish scales glints tangled

bowl round tipped over
sounds wet dripping and my feet
walk around shards of eye
glass empty the bowl glints
rolls drops smashes split opened

inside of me moving
immersed submerged in water
the way the tide fills
my stomach i am reminded
of pink wide eye fishes

inside first floor at the
randomization factory

secrete

sits type chair

have sown
marbles
statue
steel polished
scratch magenta
face

strangle
carbide mouth bits

carbon silhouette dated
fossil oil dresses

foyer signs pointing eyelashes

neck welt
amber smash parade
sticks wrought sigh trilobite

up way elevate down again stair

whisper slapping
back seat

wash

puddles
petal
sulked medallion

copy wave

print heat storm

            emboss four steps

            fractal lettertree
                        paradigm

            grew
            glue
            sticky
                        so
sticky
glued arm back on waitress pink statue
ette

tool box

plastic lip bite polymer
walk
        grate
        gyrate
        grate
        sandpaper
and slippery uncollected
sweet mouth prickly
vinegar tongue

pause and the machines grind sound

tilt back
drink fall
back
reds yellow dry leaf

flip shop

groaning upstretch start

press tetrahedron

smile
feel bone
lipstick
smeared print
fingers

light scream fast catch

hail platform salute eye dripping

wear shoe sandcastles
sergeant dilemma mile

union left right sew together

malleable

press

fingers
one
five
hard

walls feel
hardness
cool drywall
yielding
juice

pollute

erect cloud swallow

window screen pile construction
air suburb

ripen
fold

lip wrap
welt wet spit
fabric chair

arrest tighten
slips knot slip

sixteen lengths
tied wool
table wood
                knot

rooms and corners

plant fills

with breath noise red
        and lily of the valley and
        heliotrope split
fibres swimming
proud of wraps tangles
and fragmented
shape

and capture swallows in cans
store refrigerate insect names
pinned to feet
and abdomen

fingers
pressing sing
with sounds

whisper cars and houses

        home house without
        smallness and
        me
        and
        small me

corners

cabinets in cupboards
            peer out behind
            child and forks
            see   wailing at statues
            wave to falling smash the

            fragments meeting and painting
            eye stained strain

skeletal we
parts
picked apart
on front lawns

&me

shape changing

cotton the walls and
clock arm narrow
work pacing
the oblique vendor
coloured signs
            wander blue
            yellow crack

postcards out
in the street birds
                        circle

birds circle
birds cold no

jacket bending
weather turn left
steep dandelion

tea melting soft
hills and digging
to paint
substance on rock

sides purple sing
on round song to
taxis

bread
in pockets
hot and soft

hats scream objectified
acknowledge day

wood

box

lip

plaster

roof

dance peeling
rind evaporate
salt boiling lashes
directly
heat eyes
looking at
dry hands

spraypainting
sides of
stop trains scale asphalt
curb   seduced posture

feather bound
wind with flower
cups reflected
in mirrors

hair braided
circled with flies

pictures passed
shadowed in lamp
forms
and mixing eager
compression

milk filled
swim no
shallow
pools one

oil red
shine paced
song bottled
sweet

                    fingers gray
people corner point
bricks
built sand cry

jewels broken
through stained glass
bells ringing and grown
thrown out
gold
and ink clothes

mineral
paper buses
drop flat
street slid white

face
quiet right expensive

miracles soft
padded angora
noon hides
warm blanket
lancing walls
behind bed

racks
collapsed stretch skin
shore

citrus boxed
on winter

water sucked
in body

billboarded
up rains orange

water years

islands swallow sky swallow

weeds erected
dug with spoons
metal
tempered
pressed to leaf

cleaning
seeds of a green

dress
pink
geranium points
hymn

the main characters

he walked towards me his hands in wooden boxes
she walked towards him her sandals paper boxes
i put my pencil down in a cardboard box

she came forward her hips weighted with steel boxes
he followed her his words trapped in a wicker box
i took inventory of the objects in my music box
he wandered around shook hands with the pink
        ballerina in the jewelry box

she tripped
he tripped over her
i got up to help   my feet tied

the boxes fell on the ground the lids open the
        contents swarming

the bees flew in touched us sticky with honey
and carried away the boxes

leaving arms
full of miscellaneous tangled objects

artichoke

peeling off the
consecutive
leaves buttered of
an artichoke
out poured
            postcards
            milk
            frames
            ball bearings
            sandcastles
            arms
            salmon
            flashlights
            round faces
            swollen lips
            microscopes
            june beetles
            ice
            pennies

with a round silver spoon i quickly ate
juice dripping down my chin
and my stomach bobbing
with the chewed up pieces
of spaces and me

street moving

i stand on the street moving
moving the street
moving

and i walked
towards you
my sounds moving
wrapping around
your waist
and your arms moving
waving at me

step into the traffic
moving the train moving

the city moving
the people moving
my breath moving

my stomach moving
as i inhale
exhale
and move quickly
to catch
the quick moving
subway home

pantry

small round bottle metal lid
inside: four arms one with a silver ring

tall narrow vinegar bottle corked
inside: pieces of glass all green

hexagonal jar paper tied over opening
inside: eyelashes olives sandpaper

tin with lid peeled half open
inside: rocketship with engine running

cracker box open side ripped
inside: crumbs and paper airplanes

tipped over bottle neck broken
inside: moist breath

margarine container lid cracked
inside: me crouching with sing song roaches

and dust lines the shelves
with wallpaper

cure for tea

the cup is warm
on a clean counter
a tea bag
dripping
wet with steam

and drinking the green
liquid slowly
not to burn
tongue

i blow on the steam
the bird floats up to the
surface
i stir
and drink
the syrupy
condensation
sugar through its beak

album

spilt
the photos mixed
with sewers
dirt
car tires
marked
mottled
with
soft histories
damage
squares granite
gravel smile
flashbulbs

playroom

life sized head inside
of doll sized home

domestic sideways
stories are
oh
oh
o
o o o
deliberately round
and
full of microscopic
moving fingers

office supplies

pencil sharpener
with shavings of my left little finger and
its nail

i bleed sharply

dark

turn the light
on
i'm drowning
in applesauce darkness holiday music and handfuls
of white touching salt stained stomachs

frames

& i looked in the frame & saw you standing with an
umbrella & you were wet through & i wondered how
long it had been raining & you asked me if i was
hungry & i pulled the clasp of my chain to the back
of my neck & looked at the billboard across the street
& peeled the clementine in my hand & some of the juice
splashed up & burned the part of the photograph where
you were laughing & you were silent & i wiped it with
citrus hands & your eyes closed & i washed the frame
with water & a warm cloth & your arm fell the umbrella too
heavy & you were wetter from the cloth & the rain & the
smell of oranges filled the doorway & i sat down & ate &
the smell is on my fingers & on my clothes & tomorrow
i'll go to the laundromat & hang the picture of you again

breakfast

i filled my mouth with frozen
cranberries
wet rounds colder red
i looked at you stopped
with mosquitoes in an
amber wall
singing along with the refrigerator
rattling
the filter stuck in my back
the antelope see-saw moving
in my marsh backyard
my arms running in front
and antlers erected
to decorate for tourists
painted my body
black and white in
squares and sat
under a spinning
lightbulb
an exhibition
for aquariums
and
sidewalk

line

in glued newspaper clipping uniforms
the assembly line whistles start
and star as socket electric light a chicken comes
down the belt
his feathers plucked and worn
tiara on feathered head
bread rolls down
the crust torn off
a book
the pages circling around ankles
in run off from the sink
the faucets were taken from
the drain clogged with
shoes
and horses
and toboggans
and wagons full of paper shapes
the children
numbered torsos and fingers
holding bouquets for
pear shaped insects
rattling in boxes
and cages
the bell sounds again
the newspaper dropped to the floor
walking through a
spinning sphere
the clock runs out
and the factory closes
for lunch
tin foil
music
and wooden men standing

angle

ten degrees/switched to on the wheels begin to move/twenty degrees/the arch bends and gears turn/thirty degrees/the room gets colder in audience expectation/forty degrees/watch is set to count/fifty degrees/a vibration moves from outside of a still life fruit basket/sixty degrees/the roundness begins and marbles roll and glass balls are erected from sound rubble/seventy degrees/standing/eighty degrees/pulleys raise immeasurable weights up to archway chandeliers and cobweb watchers/ninety degrees/the man plays operatic piano on the roof/one hundred degrees/water boils on the stove and whistles out carols/one hundred ten degrees/lights are switched off/one hundred twenty degrees/glaring off of crystal refraction prism shapes/one hundred thirty degrees/the fractal orchestra spits out/one hundred forty degrees/alphabets are thrown black and white on charcoal walls/one hundred fifty degrees/the rumbling/one hundred sixty degrees/delivery for the operator/on hundred seventy degrees/the bus stops and files in pieces inside/one hundred eighty degrees/a straight line in 3H pencil is drawn across the tiles on the floor

pointed

at the people walking by
with orange mirrors
and the fragments
of skin wrapped in
parchment
warmed in pockets
to reconstruct
their faces
screaming
to come inside
from the loud
trains
and the wind
and the
paper dolls
strung across
blue window

terrarium

lined up on the eastern facing
windowsill of her apartment
were seven mason jars
            lids perforated
            lives swarming inside
            a red glass bead balanced
            on top of each

before she went to bed
the beads put in pockets
one by one
jars dropped to floor

ceiling staring
light flash
by body
thoughts of beads
in jewelry box
rolled blue
felt edges
cut with pinking shears

years pass
marked by moving
always close eyes and
cool round red antique
beads without string
glass break against each
other in pockets
prayers exploding
our father in fingers

so quiet
water running
            over each
            over
            over
running water

monday or wednesday
now too many days
inside
woman watering
plants new
bodies hatching
underside of leaves
transparent wing
dry when awake

walls are redder
than imagined
black spots
flood pupils

attempts inventory
fail numbers
points confuse
run into themselves
red bumps
her goose flesh

held to light
red
glass beads larger
room visible
in curves
movement around
hollow spheres
indoor migration

music downstairs
a brown wing buzzing
sound continues
move in ears
cuckoo clock
synchronized
dance six feet
step hourly chime

believes
          eyes closed for decades

house
and room phones
ring in forgotten
parts sometimes after
footsteps hands
touch door
quiet knocks
without persistence

slipped over linoleum
under door
paper saves
from leaving
spot(s) unattended

bulbs cooled
refrigerator drawers
at windows
forces pale
hyacinths her
skin
windowsill leaves

no shell
flannel wrapped
crocheted afghans
damp in braids
black strand years
growth since last called

feet pad
across wood floor
do not
step on
anything red

hand now bled
into aphid factory
for food
red jewel bodies
cling grace
sing on skin

such narrow limbs
could be dissected
project tweezers
entomology pinned
to boards
a framed museum
subject under
magnification

first one
entered by accident
spots marked back
burst open
under pressure
of wings

squeeze door
frame under
not escape
lick outside
pile in hall
corners to hibernate
sneaks out
tucking under burlap

at night
yellow again
one hundred watt
balcony sunshine
beckons more
collide one another
mesmerized
yellow collapse
backs kicking
rosemary until upright

cardboard now
windows room orange
sun bends
around corrugation
suck edges
small holes form
wet breath crawls
cling to screens

make thin statues
paper cut
from newspapers
spotlit by cardboard holes
multiply daily
find homes in newsprint
skirts newly
erected heroes

lie feels
crawls extended
walk maze damp
fingerprints
circle to centre

make preserves again
home constructed
equal
    mason jars
    cats eye marbles
    a trilobite fossil
    smooth stones
    potting soil
    grass seeds
    water
    and aphids plucked
from old parsley
garden

leaning over balcony
careful not to crush
between words
pages are turned

red
spotted
without sickness
and voices
orange on counted
juice long drunk
for vocals

words too
repeat slam
into closed windows

the jars incubate
grow legs
to elevate
alphabets

hemispherical bodies
now punctuation

a language
unrolls
tongues into tap water

how many now
thousands of prayers
living penance

movements in jars

caught

i am the only
one in the
photograph
the colour
photograph the
one on the mantle
when my hair
was long
i am the only
one in the
photograph that
knows the taste
of your skin
and that is why
i am smiling

the nesting shelf

i collect
and braid
    seven feathers
    six branches
    five feet of brown string
    four pieces of carbon paper
    three blades of rye grass
    two handfuls of dryer lint
for one bird
one bird
braid for one bird
sitting plaster
on the wood shelf
above
where I nest
the one bird
braided above
me
braiding the nest
for the one bird

blue apartment

you stand in the rounded doorway
your arms upward
the walls freshly painted blue
a you aquarium
stomach wet and
blue you swim thinking
in the blue doorway

machine

the colour the colour the colour
what colour what are you asking
for which display what gallery
the room the room with the door open
your feet inside the bell ringing
loud the filings glued to your hands
and your hands glued to the wall

the wall open the door war the
smell of sugar burnt on the edges the two
sitting inside preheated looking out of the
glass the cold formed precut preheated
watchers polished together still warm
the motions of soldering iron

without picking up heels the carpet
lined the wool fallen the feet
sunk deep hands drawing geometric
shapes in glass for fish to follow the
pump moving water in cycles the air
moves up the plant leaves move
up the snail now outside a borrowed
shell a line drawn wet twice
across the floor

i watched you

swim
the pool in rooms
you transfixed on

the yellow lightbulb
suspended below the
surface

the faces reflected
above watching you
swimming

below the
surface towards
the yellow

bulb
your hair wet
down your

back eyes looking
not blinking
at the bulb

your arms
and legs moving
in the otherwise

dark rooms
of pools
where you swim

parade of dolls

come wide
vinyl eyes
through
the kitchen
and wandered

without bending
knees into
the living
room plastic
arms stop

motioned in
a polaroid
of tea
coffee
and plastic
conversation

symphony

a symbol
the sound of cymbals
splashing up
water on a
crooked to sun
houseplant

dried sweat
beaded hand
on the indentations
of a pale back

the soundtrack
otherwise
unavailable

tulip jar

the door to the
stove open the
engine started
inside the sound
exhausted by the
steam rising
the tulip jar
fastened on the
fan above
the ant gone
before the spinning
begins

your hand

walking in a cement cold
cellar low ceiling basement
rest my hand on a
round jar
your hand
inside waves to the
bulb suspended
above me

yes

voices tied in cilia
hair rolled paint
splashing
microscopic probes
touching skin
and rolling paint cilia

and yes

the movement of hair

no

am not going to fall
am not   go
to fall
are not   go
owing to fa
elle
is not
am not
will not
we are not
going to fall

green dress moving

green dress moving
in green room
hand outstretched
to touch leaves
green
of corner mildew and
cold green air
moved
through the room
passing over green
tea moving the shape
of green transparent
curtains

it is dark and
even with green eyes
open wide
the colour has
fallen to dust on
bookcase
carpet
sofa
skin
        all grey

can identify

him in the corner with grey fingers
    in the black hair hand on
    the side of his head
her with the laugh visible
    through the sounds of any
    crown of trumpets
her with blue shoes and blue sweater
    and brushes the world pink
him in trenchcoat
    pockets full of elements
    and hushed atoms
her who crashes sideways
    right foot behind left into him

and particles flying
one two three four
in the bucket under the
window molecular spots
reassembled

the scene begins again
can identify
he works in the factory

feather bed

bedding in feather
down slips
in crack
and window silt
the pot on the stove
the water boiling hot
eyes on the feathers
the stabbing beak
on the white
back traveling
in
traveling in
side

in sleep

she settles on sheets
the glass jar
with the wide mouth
open under

the bed
the water spilling out
the rocks
rolling out
the sand splashes out
the jar empty
under
the bed
the water the sand the rocks
spread
            incubate

start only

speaking voice reflected in the radio mirror
hand down mouth sewn in corners
the red sore gone and not words but sounds raising
alarm going off stopping other left right flashes
noise imposed by the turn dial narrator
smothered and unpronounceable
counting knowledge now to sigh
another week

another week
again   again

the beginning and
the supposition of a (necessary)
                                        introduction

the mouth open
the wet   oyster the pearl
balancing on   tongue
to roll off
          and be caught
to be swallowed

the pink tongue
            the pink side up of a white
                                        sided pearl

          blanket up waiting
for speeches and dialect
voices   the speech quiet
                    the eyes pointed down
            and the plane flying loud
                    full of noise
                    pointing down
without voice

begin   an introduction
of childhood
and place
and action
and oncoming
stories and traffic

moving through the
calendar   each day   another
story   another   story
another voice for beginning
another introduction
to character
and the movement on
coming
and go

the calendar

the end

it is only   the days

neon

lights trace
the shape of stomach
basement panel walls
flannel pajamas
stripped to floor

tangled and slept
breathed in
dust construction

gathered costume
fabric side glance

watched blowing glass
a round red roundness
can see through the
colour of glass
sleeping and sound
transparent

stomach pressed
against the smell
of oranges and bleach
sweating damp

in pile carpeted
basement floor

tangled shed and slept
the smell of oranges
sheets breathing when
tapping window panes
with marbles and wood

flashlight on
can see completely blue
in glass blown

winter

a mobile spins
the characters grinding
a string breaks yellow
giraffe falls quickly quickly
on the carpeted floor

winter already
i drive the windows fogged with
my breath i turn on
the radio and sing
only with travel songs

pulling a blanket
over my purple shoulders
and closing lash eyes
i peel grapes with white teeth
move roundness in my mouth

playgrounds

cannon
rock climb
statue
hood and rope hands
climbing

coming
gray tailed squirrel
running on the base
pointing fingers
running down trees and
tanks and cannon

and coming alive coming
alive coming
alive

army play
choreography
roll down
the storm

rung splashes
crouch on short grass

under cement
painted barrel
without shine

ground shush

work patience
spend weeks
try to paint dirt
multitude colours

stand on grape hyacinth
survey wrought wants
wrap fingers in clay

drink from bowl hands
sit under the
blue green
leaves of a hosta

a cloud rolls over
scream wave
continue painting

hold silver worm up to
spit sunshine
it shines
and wriggles
down

dragging paint
in curves
and whispers

exhibit

exhibit 1

a.
turbulent exercise
prolific multiplying
files of cells
monitored sketched
and alphabetized
to come together
in full movement
tremours of newness
a fusion
guard appeared
for permanent exhibition

b.
aquarium
fresh water
temperature of damp skin
lungs of water expand
expel and
no fish
but opaque glass
shards really living

c.
object department
front desk
with paper turning
catalogue
its warehouse boxed
sale of
taxonomies
one-of-a-kinds
abandoned shapes
colours
textures
some smashed

d.
locked corridor
separate and purify
base serifs under
microscopes
dissected bleed
dripping down
test tube
sides
sterilized by crew
in gloves
bottling to classify

unexpected remainders

e.
much slicing and biopsy
clamping down specimen
when ripped
it dripped slowly
and turbulently
blue dripping
onto knots
cotton thread
soundless
lines drawn tau(gh)t

f.
hammer on nail
tinsel
breakage
air floods in

hours of scurry

g.
tells stories
whispering voice
milk sweet syllables
sealed in glass jars for long-term
preservation

h.
stretched in flight
pinned to cardboard
latin name in blue
ballpoint ink
watching from frame

exhibit 2

a.
cold glass
rolled tongued
into cheek
against teeth with
click hand
picked between
front bite
wetness evaporates
into continents
some unnamed and
unspeakable

b.
even the slightest
prod leaves
ink stain
behind

c.
eyes blinded from
pureness of white
without distraction
or reflection

d.
remove stains
that cross contaminate
natural order
in storage
before the new
sentence   begins.

e.
forgotten about newspapers
stories pile at door
words ooze under
weather stripping
stick to the pads
feet when walking

f.
inkpad on sill
every hesitation
is marked
in maps
smears each
trip
and
misstep

exhibit 3

a.
creaks and pushes
grunt through cool earth
popping sounds
much unfurling
flashes
coloured light
filtered in skin
blue milk
pushing up
reassembling soil
gears grinding upwards
stretch suck
                lean
fall

b.
strike union
nothing rotated
inspected realigned
and the order
changes narrative
birthed scrap parts
overflowing trash bin
develops shape
rhythm and
self-sufficiency

c.
every stress
dimension and angle
measured and recorded
so that even the most
subtle
transgression
can be noted

d.
in the centrifuge
for refurbishing
moving parts
suspended from
in boxes
lips salty and dry
licked bitter rough

e.
branches long
extended drag
roof scratching
the sounds working

f.
metal on metal
teeth on gears touching
slightly enough
small pressure
until words are pumped out
vaseline smooth with residue
until
words

exhibit 4

a.
wash fingers
and eyes
scented soap
slight sting

b.
mixing sugar into warm water
until (words)
even its steam
is hot and sweet

c.
up legs like freckles
brushes them
subtly pushing
off
balance
in   another
          direction

d.
scrubs down
white wallpaper
bleached white much
brighter all the other points faded alphabet

e.
beads through fingers
repeatedly
with prayers
on words
matched with
touches
degrees   of belief

f.
their legs
metronome mechanical
lashes
blinks only sound
the kettle boiling

g.
trims grass
scissors sharp
blade by blade
lid fits
no bends or sap tears

h.
looks taller
stretched
out
classified
movements over
hands
link punctuated
highways

Thank Yous:

Meghan Jackson wishes to thank rob mclennan for his dedication and encouragement over the past decade; Don Summerhayes and Christopher Dewdney for invaluable advice and inspiration; her parents, Daniel and Uylond Lynch and her brother, Brendan for being devoted readers since day one; and her husband, Nick Jackson for his sense of humour, support, and love, even after all these years.

Acknowledgements:

"terrarium" was first published as a chapbook by above/ground press in March 2001.

"inside first floor at the randomization factory" originally appeared as *STANZAS* #13 (Ottawa ON: above/ground press, June 1997), and was reprinted in *Groundswell: best of above/ground press, 1993-2003* (Fredericton NB: cauldron books / Broken Jaw Press, 2003).

"exhibit" was first published in *evergreen: six new poets* (Windsor ON: Black Moss Press, 2002).

"fish: five tanka" appeared as a small chapbook by above/ground press in April 1999.

the poems "blue apartment," "the main characters," and "nesting shelf," were published as above/ground press broadsheets #107 (December 1999), #182 (published for the ottawa international writers festival, October 8, 2003), and #199 (January 2004).

About the author:

Meghan Jackson is the author of two published chapbooks and several broadsheets. Her poems have most recently appeared in the collections *Groundswell: best of above/ground press* and *evergreen: six new poets*. She currently works as an editor, knitting instructor, and pattern designer in the Greater Toronto Area. Born in Scarborough, Ontario, Meghan has lived throughout Southern Ontario in the years since, and she has finally settled down in Willow Beach, Ontario with her husband Nicholas Jackson and their two dogs, Eliot and Molly. *Movements in Jars* is Meghan Jackson's first poetry collection.